# FAILURES TURNED INTO TECH FORTUNES

## FANTASTIC FAILURES
### From Flops to Fortune

MARTIN GITLIN

## 45TH PARALLEL PRESS

Published in the United States of America by Cherry Lake Publishing Group
Ann Arbor, Michigan
www.cherrylakepublishing.com

Reading Adviser: Beth Walker Gambro, MS, Ed., Reading Consultant, Yorkville, IL
Series Adviser: Virginia Loh-Hagan
Book Designer: Frame25 Productions

Photo Credits: © raindropstudio/Shutterstock, cover, title page; © franz12/Shutterstock, 4; © Gorodenkoff/
Shutterstock, 5; © Ink Drop/Shutterstock, 7; © G-Stock Studio/Shutterstock, 8; Jawed Karim and Yakov Lapitsky, CC
BY-SA 3.0 via Wikimedia Commons, 9; © Maxisport/Shutterstock, 10; freddthompson, CC BY-SA 2.0 via Wikimedia
Commons, 11; © VDB Photos/Shutterstock, 12; Unknown author, Public domain, via Wikimedia Commons, 15; FDR
Presidential Library & Museum, CC BY 2.0 via Wikimedia Commons, 16; © Damon Carter/Shutterstock, 17;
Acroterion, CC BY-SA 3.0 via Wikimedia Commons, 18; © Esin Deniz/Shutterstock, 19; © Asia Images Group/
Shutterstock, 20; Louis Bachrach, Bachrach Studios, restored by Michel Vuijlsteke, Public domain, via Wikimedia
Commons, 23; Illus. in: Frank Leslie's illustrated newspaper, 1880, June 10, p. 353, Library of Congress, Prints and
Photographs Division, 24; Library of Congress, Prints and Photographs Division, 25; Daderot, CC0, via Wikimedia
Commons, 26; Thomas Edison's patent drawing and application for an improvement in electric lamps, patented
January 27, 1880; Records of the Patent and Trademark Office; Record Group 241; National Archives, 27; © Ground
Picture/Shutterstock, 28; Benh LIEU SONG, CC-by-SA 4.0 via Wikimedia Commons, 29; © PeopleImages.com - Yuri
A/Shutterstock, 32

**45th Parallel Press** is an imprint of Cherry Lake Publishing Group.

Library of Congress Cataloging-in-Publication Data has been filed and is available at catalog.loc.gov

Cherry Lake Publishing would like to acknowledge the work of the Partnership for 21st Century Learning, a
network of Battelle for Kids. Please visit Battelle for Kids online for more information.

Printed in the United States of America

**Note from publisher:** Websites change regularly, and their future contents are outside of our control. Supervise
children when conducting any recommended online searches for extended learning opportunities.

# Contents

# INTRODUCTION

"If at first you don't succeed, try, try again." This is an old saying. It's been said a lot. It's a great tip. Failure is part of life. It's not bad. It can have good results. People must not let failure defeat them. They should keep trying. Failing can lead to success.

Tech creators include computer scientists and engineers. They learn from their mistakes. They know about failing. They have ideas. They invent tools. They improve the way we do things.

But not all ideas work. Some ideas **flop**. *Flop* means to fail. Ideas may not work as planned. Successful people don't give up. They solve problems. They find other uses for flops. They turn flops into fortunes.

The tech world has many examples. Many great products started as failures. These failures worked out. They made life easier. They helped people at work. They helped people at home.

Successful tech creators show **persistence**. Persisting means not quitting. Their hard work paid off. That is a lesson everyone can learn.

# CHAPTER 1

# YouTube: A Failed Dating Site

The year was 2005. It was Valentine's Day. That seemed like a perfect launch date for a dating website. The website was called YouTube.

Today, YouTube is huge. But it started small. It was created by a group of friends. The creators were Chad Hurley, Steve Chen, and Jawed Karim. They were computer scientists. They were working on a computer in Hurley's garage.

Dating websites help people find love. They help people find partners. YouTube wanted to help connect people.

Users were asked to make videos. They were asked to talk about themselves. They were asked to share what they wanted in a partner.

The creators tried to make it work. They recruited women to post videos. They offered $20. They had a slogan. The slogan was, "Tune in, hook up." They used this slogan in **ads**. Ads are promotions.

The creators waited. They waited for a while. There was no action. Five days later, no one had **uploaded** a video. Uploading means to post. The creators could have given up. But they didn't. They believed in their idea. They wanted it to succeed.

They opened their minds. They were willing to make changes. They asked 2 questions. Why did they limit videos to people seeking dates? Why not open the website to anyone?

Jawed Karim (b. 1979)

Karim went to work. He was at the San Diego Zoo. He posted a video of himself. It was just 18 seconds long. He stood in front of elephants. He talked about how long their trunks were. He called it "Me at the Zoo." In 2023, it's still popular. It has more than 293 million views.

YouTube went public a month later. **Investors** trusted Hurley and Karim. Investors give money to a company. They supported YouTube.

Ronaldinho Gaucho is a retired soccer player. He's famous. Nike is a sporting goods company. It posted an ad in October 2005. The ad featured Gaucho. It was the first post to reach 1 million views. Soon YouTube reported 8 million views a day. Everyone watched YouTube videos.

The videos don't have to be important. Many are just for fun. Many are silly. One video is titled "Charlie Bit My Finger." It shows a baby biting his big brother's finger. It has nearly 1 billion views.

YouTube could be serious. It was a great way to share information. The website co-hosted a **debate** in 2007. Debates are arguments. The video featured U.S. presidential candidates. Today, YouTube is used for all kinds of things. It shares music. It shares news. It shares how-to videos. It shares much more.

YouTube hit 1 billion views a day by October 2009. Twenty hours of new videos were posted every minute. By then, Google had bought YouTube. Google is an online company. It bought YouTube for $1.65 billion.

The sale made the creators rich. Not bad for 3 guys and a failed dating site.

# FLOPPED!

## Sony Betamax Cassette Tapes

TV watching has greatly changed. Today, there are tons of channels. There's streaming. Early TV was simpler. At first, TV had to be watched live. There was new tech in the 1970s. It was exciting. Video recorders were invented. TV watchers could now tape shows. They could watch them at their own time. Two companies competed for buyers. One was Sony. It invented Betamax. The other was Japan Victor Company. It invented VHS video tapes. Both recording machines worked. But the winner was VHS. Its recorders were cheaper. They were also 7 pounds (3.2 kilograms) lighter. They became far more popular. Sony lagged far behind. It learned an important lesson. It needed to watch the competition more closely.

# CHAPTER 2

# Microwave Ovens: How Melted Chocolate Started It All

Americans were changing in the early 1970s. This was especially true for women. Before, many women did not work outside their homes. But now many were taking jobs. They had less time at home. This meant they had less time to cook big dinners. They wanted a faster way to make meals.

TV dinners had been around for 20 years. But they had to be heated on a stove or in an oven. That could take up to an hour. The microwave oven changed things. It heated meals in a few minutes. That made life easier.

Microwaves are part of our daily lives. But few people know how the microwave was invented. Its roots can be traced back to 1945. That was the last year of World War II (1939–1945). The war effort inspired **radar** technology. Radar are radio waves.

President Franklin Delano Roosevelt (1882-1945)

During the war, U.S. President Franklin Delano Roosevelt worked with Raytheon. Raytheon was a company. It made weapons of war. It worked on radar systems for ships. One of its scientists was Percy Spencer. Spencer left a chocolate bar in his pocket. He worked on a radar project. His chocolate melted. This made Spencer curious.

Spencer did some tests. He brought popcorn kernels into the radar lab. He watched them pop. The kernels exploded all over. Spencer then tried an uncooked egg in its shell. Soon the egg exploded.

Spencer knew he was on to something. He began building a special oven. In 1947, he finished the job. Raytheon produced the first one that year. The microwave oven was called the Radarange. It was first sold to restaurants. It was also used to reheat meals on airplanes.

These microwave ovens weren't ready to be in homes. They were huge. They weighed over 750 pounds (340.2 kg). They were also costly. Each sold for $5,000.

Raytheon wanted to improve the microwave. It bought Amana Refrigeration in 1965. This company made refrigerators and freezers. New technology emerged. Scientists made the Radarange smaller. This made it cheaper. The microwaves had to be **marketed**. Marketing means to promote. The goal is to sell.

A team of 42 women helped market the microwave. They showed others how to use it. They cooked bacon in it. One of the women was Jo Anne Anderson. Anderson said she didn't need to say much to sell the microwave. She said, "You don't have to. It's a marvel."

Soon microwaves were in homes across the world. They fit into people's lifestyles. Entire meals were cooked in a few minutes. This gave people more free time. Microwaves have come a long way. No more standing by hot stoves all day.

# BEHIND THE SCENES
## Questions from Congress

Microwaves were still new in the 1970s. People were used to stoves. Some people were worried. They didn't know how they worked. They didn't know much about radiation. They didn't trust new technology. They thought it could harm them. The *New York Times* caused more concern. They warned readers in 1973. They claimed microwaves were not completely safe. The U.S. Senate held hearings. Hearings are discussions. They talked about product safety. Many Americans didn't care. They liked how microwaves made their lives easier. They bought microwaves. Today, about 90 percent of U.S. homes have one. They're completely safe. And they're 100% useful.

# CHAPTER 3

# Thomas Edison and 3,000 Failed Lightbulbs

People rarely think about lightbulbs. They flick a switch. A room lights up. But that tech didn't exist for centuries. Thomas Edison helped make it happen. He did this in 1880. He failed a lot. But he didn't give up. His persistence made the world a brighter place.

Back then, arc lamps lit up streets. An arc lamp was very bright. It was also noisy. It needed a high **voltage**. Voltage is the strength of an electrical charge. It could be dangerous. It was not good for homes. Edison wanted to light up small spaces. He wanted to light up rooms. He wanted lightbulbs everyone could buy.

Other inventors had created lightbulbs. Electricity would heat a thin strip. This thin strip was called a **filament**. The filament would get hot. When hot, it would glow. Other inventors used **platinum** filaments. Platinum is a rare metal. It was too expensive. Edison needed something cheaper.

Thomas Edison (1847-1931)

He tested thousands of materials for the filament. Nothing worked. His lamps burned for only a few hours. He needed them to stay lit. That took persistence. Edison had a lot of that. He worked with other scientists. They worked all the time. They were always thinking. They tried 3,000 different ideas. All of them failed.

GENERAL VIEW OF MENLO PARK AND EDISON'S LABORATORY.

One day, Edison was sitting in his lab. He rolled a piece of **carbon**. Carbon is a chemical element. It is in all living things. Carbon is left over when living things burn. Edison **carbonized** plant pieces. To carbonize means to make something into carbon. This took a long time.

Edison carbonized cotton thread. He charged it with electricity. This worked! The thread lit up. It burned with an orange glow. It stayed bright for 15 hours.

Edison kept working. He made his discovery stronger. He found a way make light last longer. He finally invented the lightbulb lamp. He got a **patent** for it in 1880. Patents are legal rights. They protect inventors' ideas.

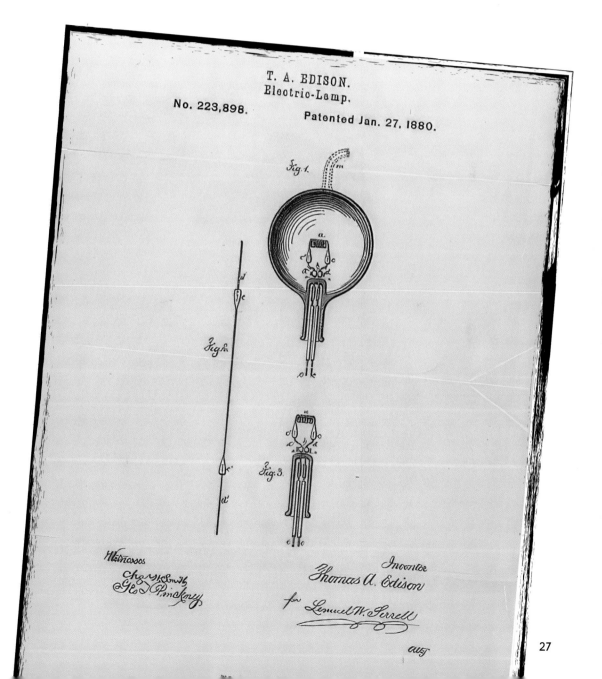

More than 140 years have passed since Edison's invention. People around the world use lightbulbs.

Edison's invention changed how people live. It let people work longer. It let them play longer. People no longer had to depend on sunlight.

# SUCCESS STORY!
## A "Sweeping" Change

The first vacuum cleaner was invented in 1860. The first electric one came out in 1908. But James Dyson was not satisfied. He wanted a better model. He thought about what was wrong with the vacuums. The problem was the bags. The bags filled with dirt. This made the vacuums not work as well. Dyson wanted to change that. He wanted to invent a bagless vacuum. He tried more than 5,000 times. He had no success. He also ran out of money. Most people would have quit. Not Dyson. His wife sold art to support the family. Dyson kept trying. He tinkered with the design. In 1983, he did it. The Dyson bagless vacuum cleaner was born. Sales soared. Dyson made billions of dollars.

# LEARN MORE

## Books

Latta, Sara L. *Microwave Man: Percy Spencer and His Sizzling Invention*. New York: Enslow Publishing, 2014.

Loh-Hagan, Virginia. *Tech*. Ann Arbor, MI: Cherry Lake Publishing, 2021.

Roberts, Dr. Jillian, and Jane Heinrichs. *On the Internet: Our First Talk About Online Safety*. Victoria, BC, Canada: Orca Book Publishers, 2022.

## Websites

With an adult, explore more online with these suggested searches.

"How Do Microwave Ovens Work?" Encyclopedia Britannica

"Thomas Edison," Easy Science for Kids

YouTube Kids

# GLOSSARY

**ads** (ADZ) advertisements, or displays of a product to convince people to buy it

**carbon** (KAR-buhn) a chemical element found in all living things

**carbonized** (KAR-buh-nyzd) made into carbon

**debate** (dih-BAYT) a public argument on issues

**filament** (FIH-luh-muhnt) a thin wire that lights or heats up when an electric current passes through it

**flop** (FLAHP) to fail

**investors** (in-VESH-stuhrs) people who lend money to a business to earn a later profit

**marketed** (MAR-kuht-uhd) promoted a product

**patent** (PA-tuhnt) government document allowing someone the sole right to make and sell an invention

**persistence** (per-SIH-stuhns) the will to keep trying after first failing or experiencing challenges

**platinum** (PLAT-nuhm) a rare metal

**radar** (RAY-dar) a device that sends out radio waves to detect an object

**uploaded** (uhp-LOHD-uhd) transferred from one electronic device to another

**voltage** (VOHL-tij) the force of an electrical charge

## INDEX

## ABOUT THE AUTHOR

Martin Gitlin is an educational book author based in Connecticut. He won more than 45 awards as a newspaper sportswriter from 1991 to 2002. Included was a first-place award from the Associated Press for his coverage of the 1995 World Series. He has had more than 200 books published since 2006. Most of them were written for students.